PANZER III

Horst Scheibert

Schiffer Military/Aviation History
Atglen, PA

Front cover artwork by Steve Ferguson, Colorado Springs, CO.
Additional research by Russell Mueller.

EGYPT DENIED
A PzKpfw III Ausf. G, of the 15th Panzer Division *Afrikakorps* (DAK) turns hard about on the perimeter of another murderous British artillery barrage. During the early battles of 1941, the PzKpfw III proved to be a most dangerous adversary in the desert. Despite their inferior numbers, PzKpfw III equipped units led the way to the capture of the British stronghold of Tobruk, Libya in early 1942. The PzKpfw III quite literally made DAK commander Erwin Rommel a *Feldmarschall.*

Translated from the German by Dr. Edward Force.

Printed in the United States of America.
ISBN: 0-88740-676-9

This book was originally published under the title,
Der Panzer der Blitzsiege, Panzerkampfwagen III,
by Podzun-Pallas Verlag.

We are interested in hearing from authors with book ideas on related topics.

Published by Schiffer Publishing Ltd.
77 Lower Valley Road
Atglen, PA 19310
Please write for a free catalog.
This book may be purchased from the publisher.
Please include $2.95 postage.
Try your bookstore first.

Foreword

Horst Scheibert, served in 1942-43 as a company chief in a Panzer unit, and drove these tanks in action many times in the attempts to relieve Stalingrad and the subsequent combat leading up to the reconquest of Kharkov.

A Panzer III in action on the steppes of southern Russia. It could still be an Ausf. J, but is presumably an Ausf. L, since the turret and side aprons were first used in great numbers on that type.

Panzerkampfwagen III Sd.Kfz.141

In 1934 the military request was made for a medium tank, which was planned as a support or command tank for Panzer I and II and given the designation of Kampfpanzer III. It was intended to have an armor-piercing tank gun, enough space for additional radio equipment, and a weight not exceeding fifteen tons. The developmental contracts were issued to the firms of MAN, Daimler-Benz AG, Rheinmetall and Krupp. When the results were tested, Daimler-Benz was favored. Its tank was armed with a 3.7 cm gun, had a five-speed gearbox, and was powered by a Maybach DSO motor producing 250 HP, which gave it a top speed of 32 kph.

The idea of equipping it immediately with a 5 cm tank gun was dropped for reasons of time, as the 3.7 cm antitank gun was available and a 5 cm gun would have had to be developed first. But the turret was designed so that it could also hold heavier armament than the 3.7 cm gun. There were also various opinions as to the number of machine guns, as well as the type of running gear. Very few German tanks were the subjects of so much experimentation as the Panzer III.

In 1936 the first tanks were already delivered to the newly organized Panzer troops. In every new series there were large or small changes. Thus the Ausf. A to E came into being during peacetime and the later F to M during the war. The technical data on the most important types will be found at the end of this book.

There were variants of all types (for example, the customary command tank).

The main differences and interesting variations between the individual types will be illustrated below in drawings.

The ventilator flaps in the front of the turret included –until Ausf. D – a vision slit. It had only two return rollers on each side – three as of Ausf. B.

Panzerkampfwagen III, Ausf. A

Right:
This was the first Panzer III built by Daimler-Benz. it had a 3.7 cm gun (L/45), three MG 34 (two in the turret, the third at the bow), and ten of them were supplied for troop testing in 1936. It is easy to recognize by the five large road wheels on each side.

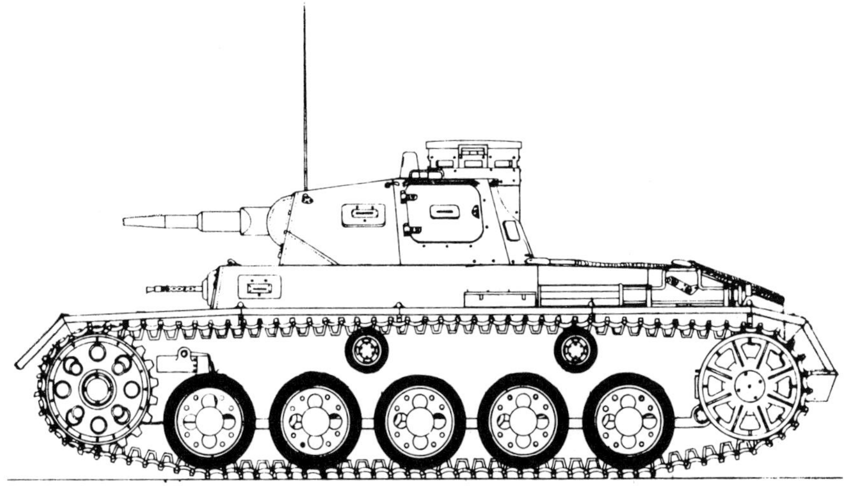

There are few photos since only ten examples were built.

Above: Ausf. L, shown to illustrate the differences from the Ausf. A shown on these pages.

Above: Another photo of the rare Panzer III, Ausf. A. The bow and the front of the turret are easy to recognize. The bow machine gun and one turret machine gun have been removed.

Below: In this photo of a parade, the rear of the Ausf. A tank is easy to recognize. At right stands Hitler with the commanders of the Army, Navy and Luftwaffe.

In the drawings of the individual basic types shown in this volume, the most important changes from the previous types have been indicated by heavy lines, arrows and textual references.

In general, though, it can be said that it is often difficult and in some cases even impossible to differentiate one version from the following or the previous type. This is because of the differences in the types, which are scarcely recognizable externally, especially when only one photo of the tank in question is available, and it does not reveal the typical differences. Most of all, reequipping with 5 cm in place of 3.7 cm guns, additional armor plate, track aprons, Rommel boxes, etc., or general overhauling involving the installation of old spare parts in newer versions and vice versa, created many new variations.

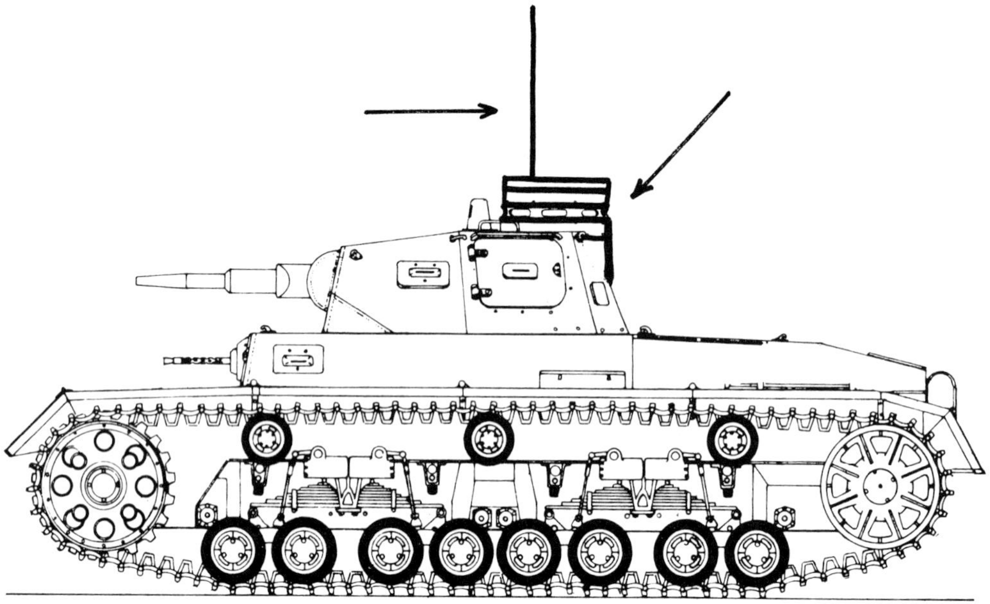

The three types, B, C and D, are easy to recognize by the arrangement of the leaf springs.

Panzerkampfwagen III, Ausf. B

Upper left: This type now has eight double road wheels and three (instead of the former two) return rollers. In addition, the commander's cupola has been changed somewhat from the previous model. The armament remained the same. Fifteen of this type were built and turned over to the troops for testing in 1937.

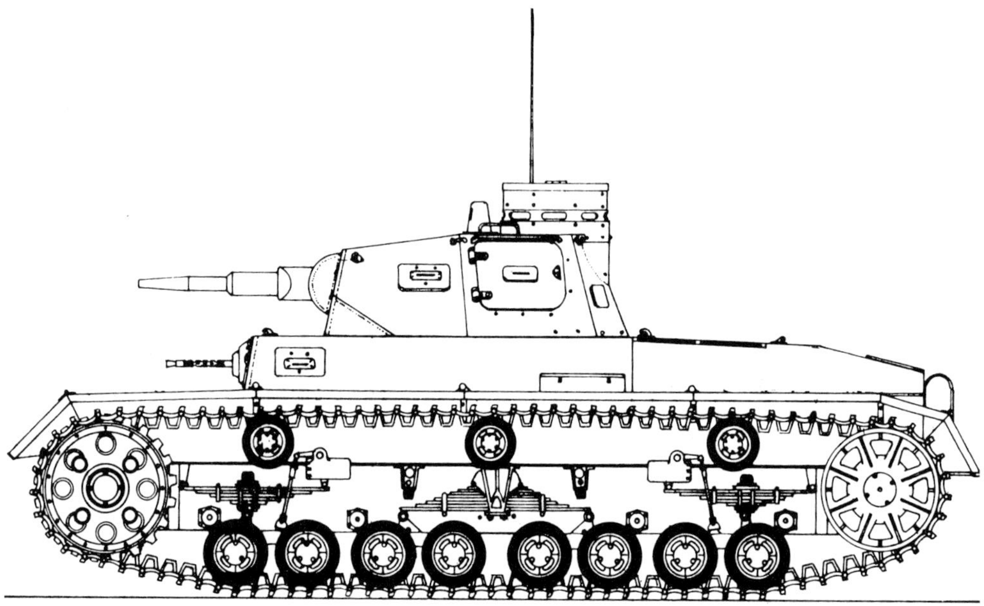

Panzerkampfwagen III, Ausf. C

Here too, the chief identifying marks are in the running gear, which now shows a different arrangement of the leaf springs (now three). Of this type too, only fifteen test models were built around the end of 1937 and the beginning of 1938.

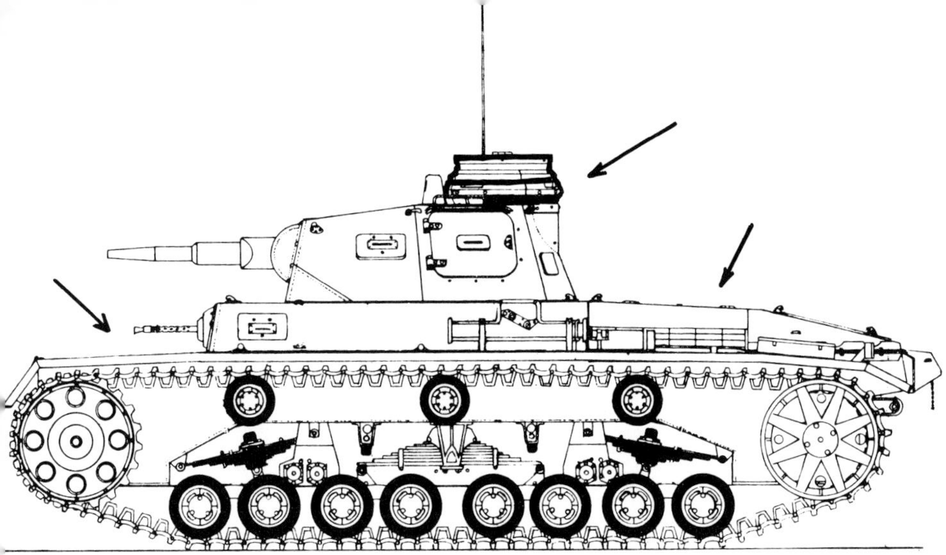

Panzerkampfwagen III, Ausf. D

Above and upper right: 55 tanks of this type were built in 1938! A further change was made to the running gear. The front and rear leaf springs are now mounted at an angle. It also was fitted with heavier armor, scarcely noticeable externally, and thus weighed almost 20 tons. In addition, the former five-speed gearbox was replaced by a six-speed type. The commander's cupola was also changed somewhat.

Right: A Panzer III of Ausf. D in the Polish campaign. In this photo it is easy to see that one of the two turret machine guns is mounted in a separate ball mantelet. The white cross customary in this campaign has had its color darkened so as not to betray the tank easily.

Here an Ausf. D Panzer III drives up the approach to a bridge during the Polish campaign (note the white cross on the turret).

Above: A Panzer III, Ausf. B in the Polish campaign – a rare photo! Below: A photo taken during Wehrmacht maneuvers in 1938. It was taken from the magazine "Die Wehrmacht" and shows an Ausf. D Panzer III standing ready.

This photo shows details of the commander's cupola of a Panzer III D. In the background is a Panzer II, probably Ausf. A.

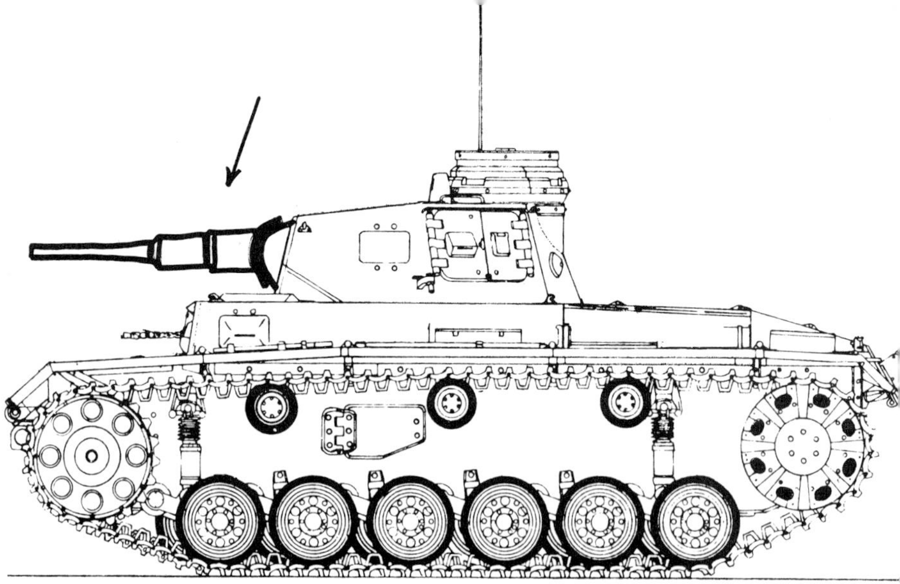

Panzerkampfwagen III, Ausf. E

Above: Here again, the running gear shows the greatest recognizable difference. It now consists of six double road wheels on swinging arms attached to torsion bars. The side entrance hatches on the turret are now divided in two. The motor was upgraded to 300 horsepower. This version reached the troops in 1939 and was the Panzer III used in the first two years of the war. About 500 of these tanks were built. Along with Daimler-Benz, they were also produced by Famo, Henschel, MAN, Wegmann and MNH. Several tanks of this type were later equipped with the 5 cm KwK (L/42). This panzer gun can be recognized by its larger caliber and longer, not conically shaped barrel, as well as by the now external roller mount.

The two photos at left show the Panzer III, Ausf. E. While this type still has two machine guns in the turret (Ausf. F only has one), Ausf. F has ventilating louvers for the front brakes at the bow, near the headlights.

Above: A Panzer III Ausf. E with a logged road section (for crossing swampy areas) on the back. While the machine gun in the driver's area is protected by a sleeve, the 3.7 cm tank gun bears a light-colored (probably makeshift) muzzle protector.

Upper right: A Panzer III Ausf. E in a destroyed French village during an advance through the Weygand Line.

Right: A Panzer III Ausf. E with a luggage carrier (Rommel box) on the turret (a rarity!). Note also the seal around the turret hatch to make it watertight during deep wading. The steel helmets indicate that this crew is experienced. There were many head injuries to crewmen who looked out of their tank.

Upper left: Driving through brick walls was a popular sport, though the resulting dust was not exactly useful. To do it, the turret was set at 6:00 position (gun to the rear).

Above: Panzer III E on a Russian road in the summer of 1941.

Left: Panzer III E tanks take positions close together, probably in a drill with live ammunition. The replacement road wheels can be seen. Their rubber wrappings were prone to damage, so they often had to be changed.

Above: A Panzer III E in rough country. It can be seen that the air ventilators in the front of the turret no longer include lookouts. On the other hand, a vertical shield protects the ventilators from frontal fire. These ventilators were used through Ausf. J.

Upper and lower right: These pictures show the simplification of the new running gear by the use of individual suspension and torsion bars. This also allowed the installation of exit hatches (between the front and middle return rollers) on both sides. The crewmen could more safely abandon a motionless tank that was under fire. In the photo at right, the locations and mounts of the machine guns can be seen.

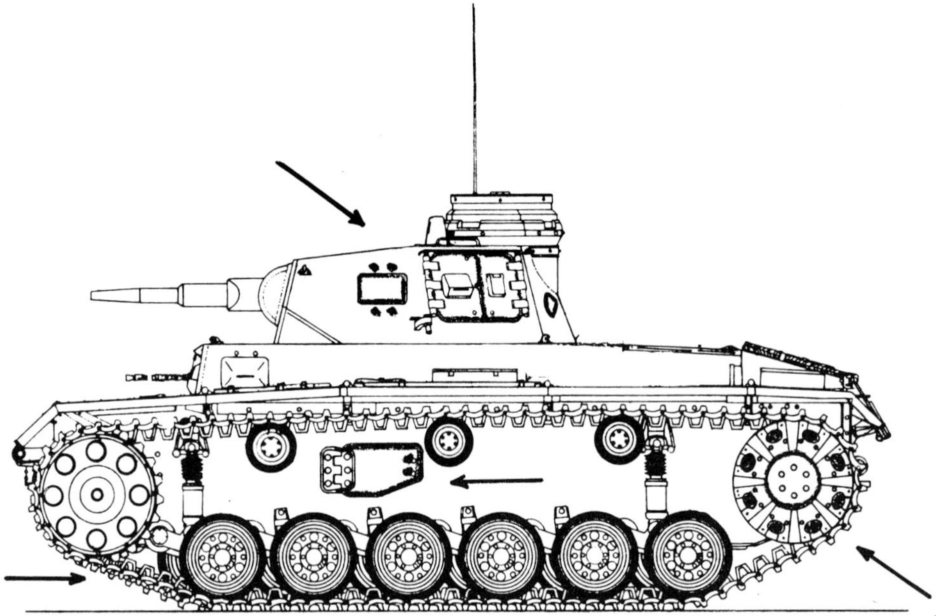

Panzerkampfwagen III, Ausf. F

Above: It differed from Ausf. E only in slight changes to the turret, the commander's cupola, and the motor. Later, along with the E, G and H types, it had additional 30 mm armor screwed onto the turret and driver's area. Almost all were also reequipped with the 5 cm KwK (L/42) gun. It was produced by the firms already named, with about 500 made in all. Along with the KwK, it, like all the subsequent models, had only one machine gun in the turret. In addition, it had ventilators for the front brakes in the bow plate.

These pictures of the Panzer III F show the death's-head emblem on the canister rack of the turret (Panzer regiment 3 in the photo above). Racks of this type – also attached to the rear and the track aprons (see picture) – existed in numerous forms.

A Panzer III F during the French campaign. The usual bucket at the rear, over the fog launcher tent canvas, spare track links and road wheels. The two stripes on the turret are the unit's marks of recognition. At left is a gathering place for captured French soldiers. Note also the white license plate on the "civilian" car. The letters mean Wehrmacht, Heer, Propaganda-Kompanie. It is probably the car of the photographer who took this picture.

A Panzer III F with an unofficial unit emblem on the lower part of the commander's cupola. From Ausf. G on, this extension on the back no longer existed. The periscope on top of the turret (visible between the commander and the crewman on the left) also shows that this is an Ausf. F; Ausf. G no longer had this small tower. The fog launcher is loaded.

A very interesting picture, for it shows how hard it is to tell Ausf.s F and G apart when the back of the turret is not visible. By the brake ventilators at the front and the periscope on the turret, the tank in front is neither E nor G, yet the commander's cupola is that of the Ausf. G. The tank behind it also has a G cupola, and since it lacks a periscope, it could be taken to be an Ausf. G. Yet the 3.7 cm KwK denies this, since all Ausf. G tanks were built with the 5 cm KwK, as was the third tank. Since the ventilator atop the turret of the third tank is in an unusual spot, it can be assumed that all these tanks have been overhauled. In such cases, new parts were often installed in older tanks.

5 cm KwK (L/42)

Above: A Panzer III F (with commander's cupola) or III G (with ventilators) in North Africa.

Upper right: A Panzer III F (with commander's cupola and 3.7 cm KwK) without periscope. It carries a Rommel box on the turret, a corduroy road section in the rear, and a spare can of gasoline. Number 101 means the chief's tank of the first company.

Right: The 5 cm KwK, F-type commander's cupola and front armor plate characterize this Panzer III.

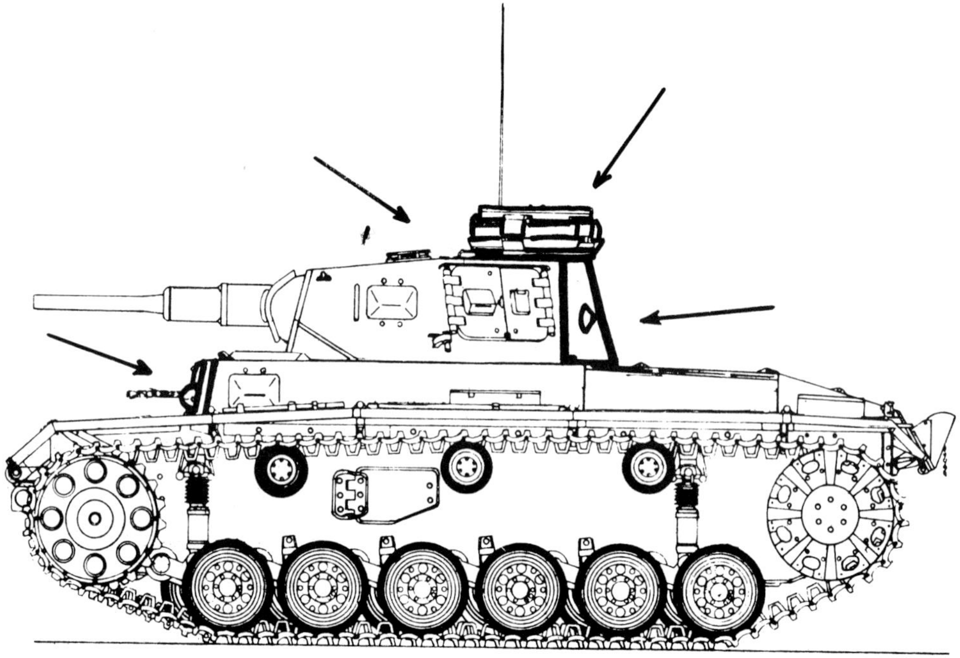

Panzerkampfwagen III, Ausf. G

Above: It had a completely new commander's cupola. The turret sides were lengthened so it no longer cut into the rear wall of the turret. This is the first version, which was built almost exclusively with the 5 cm KwK (L/42). About 900 of them were produced in 1941-42.

Upper and lower left: The commander's cupola and 5 cm KwK of these two tanks suggest that they are Ausf. G.

An Ausf. G with winter camouflage paint in Russia, in the winter of 1941-42. Note also the propeller-driven cabin sled – here, to be sure, drawn by horses.

Upper left: This is how high a Panzer III G can be lifted.

Above: A Panzer III G of the Afrika Korps (note the palm emblem in the driver's area).

Left: A Panzer III G with welded-on additional armor (30 mm) ahead of the driver.

Above: An Ausf. G moving fast on the Ukrainian steppes.

Right: It cannot be told from this photo whether this tank is a re-equipped E or F or a new G or H. But it shows interesting details of the turret front.

Below: The division symbols of the 16th, 17th and 18th Panzer Divisions.

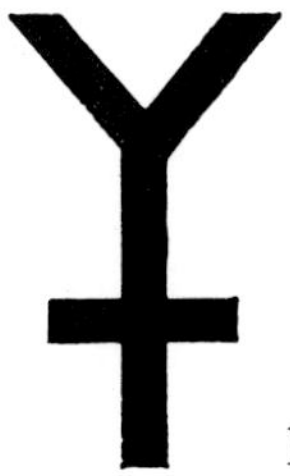

16. P. D.

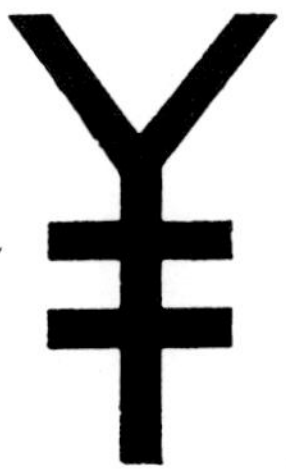

17. P. D.

18. P. D.

Upper left: Tank and grenadiers on the south Russian steppes. By the drive wheel (round instead of oval holes) this is an Ausf. G.

Upper right: An interesting mixture of various types:
– Commander's cupola: F
– Periscope: A-F
– Ventilators: G and following
– 5 cm KwK, mostly G and following
– Welded-on 30 mm front armor: done to individual tanks, Ausf. E and following.

Left: A reequipped E or F? A production G, H or J? If the commander's cupola is a valid sign, it is Ausf. E or F.

Above: A Panzer III G captured by the British before Tobruk in 1941.

Upper right: Parts of Panzer Regiment 3 (2nd Panzer Division) preparing for a parade in Athens in 1941. At left front a G, right (with diamond symbol) an F with G commander's cupola.

Right: A shot-up Panzer III G in Russia in 1942. The opened hull hatch suggests that crewmen were able to get out of the tank.

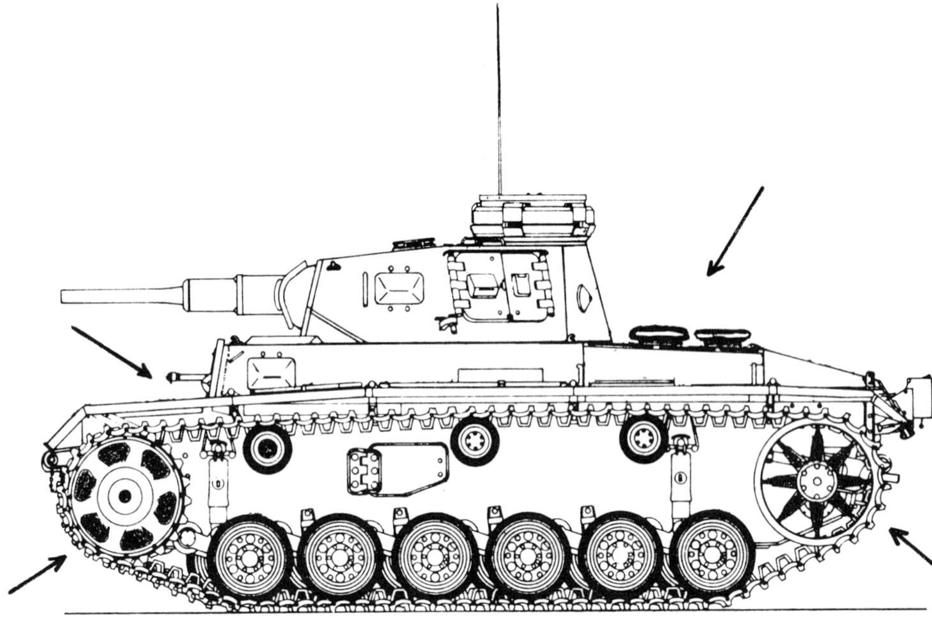

Panzerkampfwagen III, Ausf. H

Above: It was sent to the troops in great numbers in 1941. Its main differences were in the drive train (a simple alternating drive) and running gear (including steel drive wheels in spoked form, changeable gear rings, wider tracks, a return roller nearer to the drive wheel). About 1400 of them were built.

Left: A Panzer III, Ausf. H (note the new running gear, "front" return roller and bow machine gun in rectangular frame) being repaired in the field. Note the hoist between the trees. The tanks belong to the 4th Division (note division symbol on the Panzer II C in front).

Above: A Panzer III H in Africa, with a burning truck in the background. It is clearly recognizable as an Ausf. H by the shape of the drive and leading wheels. Since the bow machine gun is not recognizable, it could also be an Ausf. J. But since the latter was usually equipped with the long 5 cm KwK (L/60), it is more probable that this is an Ausf. H.

Right: An Ausf. H moving fast in North Africa. These clouds of dust betrayed the tanks' movements very quickly, especially to air reconnaissance. Note the rack for fuel canisters at the rear.

This and the following pages almost certainly depict Panzer III, Ausf. H tanks. All have the 5 cm KwK, the new drive and leading wheels, as well as the protruding front roller and the new commander's cupola.
The upper left picture shows a built-on luggage rack; the picture above shows sandbags on the turret roof, and the photo at left illustrates the typical spearhead formation: two tanks side by side, so as to provide greater firepower against the enemy if necessary.
The division symbols of the 19th, 20th and 21st Panzer Divisions are illustrated below.

19. P. D.

20. P. D.

21. P. D.

Above: Panzer III H at the harbor of Sevastopol. These tanks also bear makeshift luggage racks on the turret.

Upper right: Two Panzer III tanks in front, Panzer II and then Panzer III in back. All have been camouflaged with liquid chalk for the winter.

Right: For the sake of comparison, here is a "Zwitter" Panzer III with 5 cm KwK (L/42), commander's cupola, new-type drive wheel, advanced roller, and old-type leading wheel.

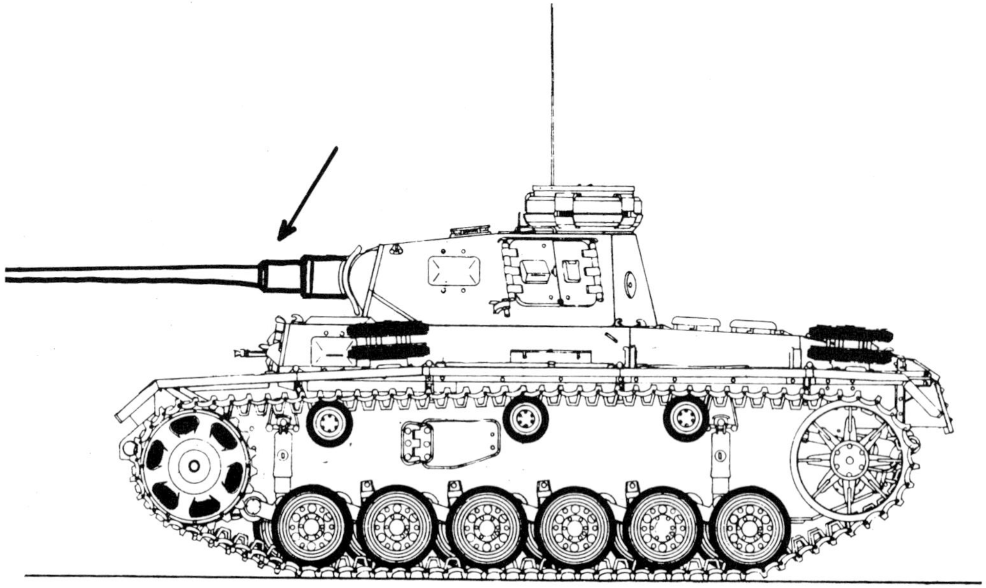

Panzerkampfwagen III, Ausf. J

Left: The long-awaited long-barreled 5 cm KwK (L/60) gun was finally installed in this version. Only the first few tanks of this type had the older, shorter 5 cm KwK. At the same time, the basic armor plate was thickened from 30 to 50 mm. With its new higher muzzle velocity and resulting greater firepower, as well as its heavier armor, it was at least equal to its opponent, the T-34. For the first time, this version included an external luggage rack on the turret (also added to some earlier types) as standard equipment. The thicker armor required a new ball mantelet for the bow machine gun and new lookouts. Of it and the following L and M types, about 2000 tanks were built from 1941 to 1943.

Upper and lower left: Panzer III Ausf. J, easily recognized by the new ball mantelet of the bow machine gun.

Above: A Panzer III J of the 3rd Panzer Division. It is easy to see how the spring-mounted antenna is moved aside when the turret turns.

Upper right: Here a Soviet "crew" is sitting on a Panzer III J. The tracks, two centimeters wider, that were introduced with Ausf. G are easy to see here.

Panzer III J and soldiers of the 5th Jäger Division fall in for action (Operation Brückenschlag) in the Demyansk pocket.

Above: Another Panzer III J with added armor plate but without aprons, which the lack of racks suggests it never had.

Upper left: A rare picture! Panzer III J with the added armor plate on the front of the hull and turret, usually used only as of Ausf. L, and the long 5 cm KwK (L/60). It also features the "aprons" around the turret and hull to ward off hollow-charge shells, standard only as of 1943. Here we see part of Panzer Regiment 1 (1st Panzer Division).

Left: A Panzer III captured in North Africa and on display in Britain. The meaning of the squares on the turret is unknown.

Above: Panzer III J in action on the South Russian steppes.

Upper right: A well-camouflaged Panzer III J of the 5th Panzer Division (note division symbol at the right front).

Right: Panzer III J tanks of Panzer Regiment 2 (16th Panzer Division). The new ball mantelet for the bow machine gun is easy to see.

Panzer III, Ausf. J, with 5 cm KwK (L/60)

These two pages show the Panzer III J with the long 5 cm KwK (L/60). On the opposite page are tanks of Panzer Regiment 11 (6th Panzer Division), on this page those of Panzer Regiment 24 (24th Panzer Division). The main differences from Ausf. L are: Ausf. L lacks the side ventilator flaps in the turret, and L usually has added armor plate and side aprons. How could it be otherwise? Ausf. J also exists without vent flaps (the last series built), and J and earlier types exist with added armor plate and side aprons. Note the different types of ventilator flaps. Those on the left page are smooth, those on this page have lookout slits. This difference was also found in earlier versions.

Above: It was used as a massed medium tank in the early years, until 1942, especially together with grenadiers. As of 1943 the Panzer IV and Panther (Panzer V) displaced it more and more.

Upper left: Its armor plate was 50 mm thick in the most vital places, 30 mm everywhere else. It could carry 84 rounds of ammunition for the 5 cm KwK (L/60), but often even more were simply piled on the ground beside it.

Left: The additional armor plate with track links on it was not without danger, for the link structure and the soft metal made shells less likely to bounce off.

Above: These Panzer III J tanks are ready to be shipped out of the Maschinenfabrik Augsburg-Nüenberg (MAN).

Right: Panzer III J in action against enemy tanks on the steppes west of Stalingrad in 1942.

Above: A look into the commander's cupola. Looking out is Leutnant Tegethoff of the 1st Company, Panzer Regiment 11. The padding between and around the Kinon blocks of the lookouts is easy to see. At left is the shaft of the anti-aircraft machine gun.

Opposite page: A Panzer III J in Africa. Its turret is set at 7:00. On the commander's cupola is an attachment for an anti-aircraft machine gun.

Upper right: The symbols of the 22nd, 23rd and 24th Panzer Divisions.

Right: A very interesting photo of a Panzer III J with "eastern tracks." Links are also hanging on the bow. They could not be used during rail transport, and in uneven country they came off easily, but they were very useful in snow.

22. P. D.

23. P. D.

24. P. D.

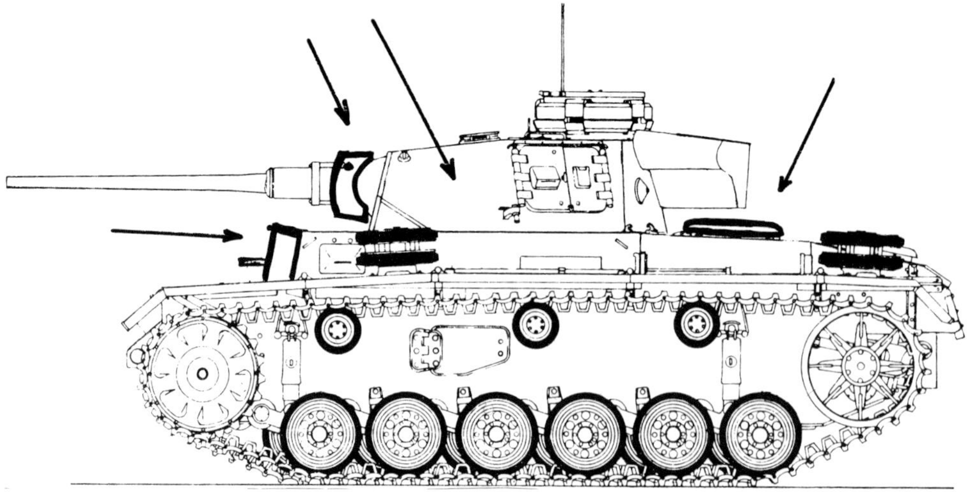

Panzerkampfwagen III, Ausf. L

The new Ausf. L was first delivered early in 1942. It is easily recognized by the relocated extra armor ahead of the gun mount in the turret and ahead of the driver. This additional armor had a thickness of 20 mm. The resulting front-end weight increase for the tank was dealt with by adding equalizing springs or a weight at the rear. This vehicle had a fighting weight of 23 tons.

Upper left: A Panzer III L. Its added armor plate is easy to see, as is the absence of ventilator flaps on the front of the turret. It carries launchers for fog cartridges.

Left: Front view of a Panzer III L. The anti-aircraft machine gun attached to the turret is easy to see. During technical service too, it was always ready for action.

All three photos very probably show Panzer III Ausf. L tanks. One is never completely sure, since the last Ausf. J series no longer had side ventilator flaps on the turret either, and additional armor plate was installed on earlier types as well, though in both cases only small numbers of tanks were involved. The three tanks shown here lack the additional armor plate on the turret, though the attachments for it are visible already. The reason is usually the lack of equalizing weights (or additional springs) in the turret. Without them, the tank gun was not usable with added armor plate. In action, though, these plates were often lost to enemy fire.

Above: Here is a column of tanks without aprons. Since the sidewalls of the turrets cannot be seen clearly, it is somewhat uncertain whether these are Ausf. L tanks.

Upper left: Panzer III as it saw its last action in 1943: Ausf. L, with 5 cm KwK (L/60), and looking like an armored knight on horseback with its side aprons.

Left: Technical service to vehicle and weapon, and time to clean and patch uniforms; all the crewmen are shown on their tank.

Above: A Panzer III L at the harbor of Toulon, near the sunken French fleet.

Upper right: A Panzer III L column. The first tank lacks additional armor plate in front of the gun mount; the second tank has it.

Right: Panzer III L being transported from Brittany to the Kalmuck Steppes in November 1942. They belong to the author's company (6th Company, Panzer Regiment 11, 6th Panzer Division). The hay bales were sent to supply horsedrawn troops at the rail terminal. Here too, not all tanks have additional armor plate.

Upper left: The front Panzer III L still has an apron on its left side; the right one has already fallen victim to enemy fire.

Above: Under the barrel of the 5 cm KwK are, left to right, Lieutenant Fuchs, Oberst Lorenz and Hauptmann Petereit of the Grossdeutschland (GD) Panzer Division.

Left: This tank, followed by an SPW, also has only bent attachments for its missing right apron.

Above: The funeral procession of the commander of the 7th Panzer Division, Generalmajor Schulz, who fell on January 28, 1944, including a white-painted Panzer III L. Since Panzer III tanks were no longer manufactured after August 1943, this is probably one of the last.

Upper right: Infantrymen riding on Panzer III L (though we cannot be 100% sure). Better a bumpy ride than a long walk, and besides, one always felt somewhat safer in the vicinity of some tanks.

Right: Because of the added armor plate and aprons, this is very probably an Ausf. L. The drive wheel is a very old type. The II on the turret skirt indicates the second unit and shows that this tank belongs to the staff.

Panzerkampfwagen III, Ausf. M

This tank, also built in 1942, differed from the Ausf. L only in having a modified exhaust system. The change gave the vehicle a wading capability of 1.30 meters. As of 1943, this version and –when still available – earlier types as well were fitted with armored aprons on both sides of the hull and the turret for protection against antitank weapons, particularly hollow-charge shells.

In particular, it dominated events in the lightning war in Poland, France, the Balkans, North Africa and Russia in 1941 and 1942. As of 1943, more and more of these tanks were replaced by the Panzer IV. Despite being upgunned to a long 5 cm tank gun, its armament had become ineffective against heavy tanks. In hindsight, the development of two similar battle tanks (III and IV) was a mistake of German tank construction. Their differences were too slight to have any significance. Only with the Panther (Kampfpanzer V), and before that with the Geschützwagen III and IV, did this double-track system come to an end. After that, new designs would include only the light Panzer II (Luchs), medium Panzer V (Panther) and heavy Panzer VI (Tiger). Though the Panzer IV was still built until the end of the war, this was done to make use of available production capacities as well as its level of development, which was still higher than that of the Panther.

All in all, the Kampfpanzer III was a reliable, fast, mobile vehicle that gave its crews enough room to operate it and provided good radio equipment. In its day – until the advent of the KW-1 and T-34 (1941) – it was equal, if not superior, to all enemy tanks; later, on account of its small-caliber gun and thin armor plate, it became more and more inferior. Its construction was thus halted, with only a few derivatives and – very particularly – the Sturmgeschütz III remaining in production.

Thus in terms of numbers, fighting value and success, it remained the tank of the Blitzkrieg. In all, over 6000 of these tanks were built.

Above and below are two pictures of the same Ausf. M tank, with an interesting, individually built luggage rack on the rear.

Technical Data of the Panzer III, Ausf. L

Motor: make & type	Maybach HL 120 TRM, Ausf. A
Cylinders	12, 60-degree V
Bore	105 mm
Stroke	115 mm
Displacement	11,867 cc
Compression ratio	6.2-6.5 : 1
RPM normal/maximum	2600/3000
Horsepower	265/300
Power to weight	14.0 HP/ton
Valve type	dropped
Main bearings	7 roller
Carburetors	2 Solex 40 JFF II
Firing order	1-12-5-8-3-10-6-7-2-11-4-9
Starter	Bosch BNG 4/24 ARS 129 + AL/ ZMD/R 9
Generator	Bosch GTLN 600/12-1500
Batteries	2 12-volt, 105 Ah
Fuel pumps	2 Solex mechanical + 1 electric
Cooling	water
Clutch	3-plate dry F & S La 120/HDA
Gearbox	ZF SSG 77 Aphon
Number of gears	6 forward, 1 reverse
Drive wheels	front
Drive axle ratio	1 : 4 (geared)
Range	road 155, off-road 95 km
Steering	Daimler-Benz/Wilson clutch-type
Turning circle	5.85 meters
Suspension	12 transverse torsion bars
Lubrication	high-pressure
Brake system	Daimler-Benz
Brake type	mechanical
Brake shoes	internal
Foot brake on	drive wheels
Hand brake on	drive wheels
Wheel types	road wheels 520/95-398, return rollers 310/70-203
Track	2510 mm
Length of tracks	2860 mm, type Kgs 61/400/120
Width of tracks	400 mm, 93 links per track
Ground clearance	385 mm
Overall length	5560 mm, KwK, 6412 mm in all
Overall width	2950 mm
Overall height	2500 mm
Firing height	1900 mm
Ground pressure	0.94 kp/sq.cm
Chassis weight	15,800 kp
Allowable gross weight	21,300 kp
Load limit	1500 kp
Seats	5
Fuel consumption	182 liters/100 km
Oil consumption	depends on use
Fuel capacity	320 liters
Armor: hull front	50 + 20 mm
hull sides	30 mm
hull rear	50 mm
turret front	50 + 20 mm
sides + rear	30 mm
Performance:	
Climbing ability	30 degrees
Ascending ability	600 mm
Wading ability	800 mm
Spanning ability	2000 mm
Armament	1 50 cm KwK 39 L/60 (78) = 2 MG 34 (4950 rounds)

5 cm KwK L/42 or L/60?